THE POETRY OF OSMIUM

The Poetry of Osmium

Walter the Educator

Silent King Books

SILENT KING BOOKS

SKB

Copyright © 2024 by Walter the Educator

All rights reserved. No part of this book may be reproduced in any manner whatsoever without written permission except in the case of brief quotations embodied in critical articles and reviews.

First Printing, 2024

Disclaimer
This book is a literary work; poems are not about specific persons, locations, situations, and/or circumstances unless mentioned in a historical context. This book is for entertainment and informational purposes only. The author and publisher offer this information without warranties expressed or implied. No matter the grounds, neither the author nor the publisher will be accountable for any losses, injuries, or other damages caused by the reader's use of this book. The use of this book acknowledges an understanding and acceptance of this disclaimer.

dedicated to all the chemistry lovers, like myself, across the world

OSMIUM

In the heart of Earth's deep, dark embrace,

OSMIUM

Where silence reigns in hidden space,

OSMIUM

There dwells a metal, rare and bold,

OSMIUM

A tale of Osmium yet untold.

OSMIUM

In shadowed mines where miners toil,

OSMIUM

Beneath the ground, beneath the soil,

OSMIUM

Osmium sleeps, a quiet king,

OSMIUM

Unseen, unheard, yet shimmering.

OSMIUM

Its atoms dance in crystal lattice,

OSMIUM

A symphony of molecular praxis,

OSMIUM

With valence shells that hold the key,

OSMIUM

To its elusive chemistry.

OSMIUM

Osmium, Osmium, oh noble element,

OSMIUM

Inert and stoic, yet so potent,

OSMIUM

With density surpassing all,

OSMIUM

A weighty crown, a heavy thrall.

OSMIUM

In alloys forged with iridium's gleam,

OSMIUM

It lends its strength, a steadfast beam,

OSMIUM

To tools of science, art, and war,

OSMIUM

A silent partner, forevermore.

OSMIUM

But Osmium holds secrets deep,

OSMIUM

In its core, mysteries to keep,

OSMIUM

For within its metallic sheen,

OSMIUM

Lies a darkness seldom seen.

OSMIUM

A toxic vapor, deadly fume,

OSMIUM

Released when heated, spells its doom,

OSMIUM

A cautionary tale, a whispered warning,

OSMIUM

Of Osmium's hidden, silent mourning.

OSMIUM

Yet in the beauty of its form,

OSMIUM

In the brilliance of its storm,

OSMIUM

There lies a majesty, a grace,

OSMIUM

A testament to nature's embrace.

OSMIUM

So let us marvel at its sight,

OSMIUM

This metal of the darkest night,

OSMIUM

For in its depths, we find a spark,

OSMIUM

A glimpse of nature's wondrous art.

OSMIUM

Osmium, Osmium, oh enigmatic soul,

OSMIUM

In your depths, we find our role,

OSMIUM

To explore, to wonder, to understand,

OSMIUM

The mysteries of this ancient land.

OSMIUM

And though your secrets may remain,

OSMIUM

Locked within your silent domain,

OSMIUM

We'll cherish you, Osmium, evermore,

OSMIUM

A symbol of the Earth's rich lore.

OSMIUM

ABOUT THE AUTHOR

Walter the Educator is one of the pseudonyms for Walter Anderson. Formally educated in Chemistry, Business, and Education, he is an educator, an author, a diverse entrepreneur, and he is the son of a disabled war veteran. "Walter the Educator" shares his time between educating and creating. He holds interests and owns several creative projects that entertain, enlighten, enhance, and educate, hoping to inspire and motivate you.

Follow, find new works, and stay up to date
with Walter the Educator™
at WaltertheEducator.com

www.ingramcontent.com/pod-product-compliance
Lightning Source LLC
LaVergne TN
LVHW010619070526
838199LV00063BA/5205